Can I tell you about Autism?

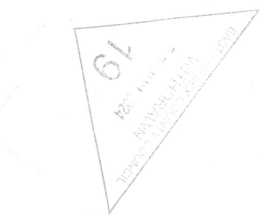

Can I tell you about...?

The "Can I tell you about...?" series offers simple introductions to a range of limiting conditions and other issues that affect our lives. Friendly characters invite readers to learn about their experiences, the challenges they face, and how they would like to be helped and supported. These books serve as excellent starting points for family and classroom discussions.

Other subjects covered in the "Can I tell you about...?" series

ADHD

Adoption

Asperger Syndrome

Asthma

Cerebral Palsy

Dementia

Diabetes (Type 1)

Dyslexia

Dyspraxia

Epilepsy

ME/Chronic Fatigue Syndrome

OCD

Parkinson's Disease

Selective Mutism

Stammering/Stuttering

Tourette Syndrome

Can I tell you about Autism?

A guide for friends, family and professionals

JUDE WELTON
Foreword by Dr Glenys Jones
Illustrated by Jane Telford

Jessica Kingsley *Publishers*
London and Philadelphia

First published in 2014
by Jessica Kingsley Publishers
73 Collier Street
London N1 9BE, UK
and
400 Market Street, Suite 400
Philadelphia, PA 19106, USA

www.jkp.com

Library of Congress Cataloging in Publication Data
Welton, Jude, author.
Can I tell you about autism? : a guide for friends, family
and professionals / Jude Welton ; foreword by
Glenys Jones ; illustrated by Jane Telford.
pages cm. -- (Can I tell you about--?)
Audience: Ages 7+
Includes bibliographical references.
ISBN 978-1-84905-453-9 (alk. paper)
1. Autism in children--Juvenile literature. I. Telford,
Jane, illustrator. II. Title. III. Series: Can I tell you
about-- ? series.
RJ506.A9W442 2014
618.92'85882--dc23
2013048193

British Library Cataloguing in Publication Data
A CIP catalogue record for this book is available from the British Library

ISBN 978 1 84905 453 9
eISBN 978 0 85700 829 9

Printed and bound in Great Britain by Bell & Bain Ltd, Glasgow

Contents

Foreword

Until recently, much of the literature has focused on sharing the diagnosis with parents and carers. Relatively little attention has been given to explaining the diagnosis to the child. Accounts from adults with autism and Asperger syndrome have suggested that being told their diagnosis is largely positive and beneficial. They report that this helps to make sense of themselves and to understand the behaviour of others, and enables them to develop strategies to manage situations they find problematic. Sharing the diagnosis also allows individuals to access relevant literature and to make contact with others with autism or Asperger syndrome. Those who feel confident and positive about their diagnosis are likely to fare better than those who know little or who have a negative view of autism.

This book is therefore very welcome, as it adds to the literature on the topic and provides a framework to use when discussing the diagnosis of autism with a child. The age at which the diagnosis should be shared is often debated and some professionals have said that it is easier to share the diagnosis when children are younger – in the primary years – than when they are teenagers or adults. This book is written for the younger age group. The first part is written as if it is spoken by Tom, a child with autism, explaining what he does and why. The second part is written for parents, carers and professionals and gives strategies, ideas and resources which may be helpful.

This book could also be used to help other children – brothers and sisters or classmates – to understand autism. For both areas of work, it is essential that the parents have given their consent and that the child is also willing and ready to be involved and/or to share the diagnosis with other children. This is skilled and sensitive work. Teaching staff and other practitioners should always shadow a person who has already done this type of work successfully, until they are confident they have the skills and understanding to do this themselves. In addition, it would be very useful to use some examples of what the child concerned does or says (to add to or replace some of the issues experienced by Tom).

A key element of this work – be it sharing the diagnosis with the child or raising peer awareness of autism – is that a positive picture of the child and of autism is promoted. In addition, it is important to demonstrate that there are good reasons why the child acts as he or she does, which then underpin and justify the reasons why adjustments need to be made at home and at school to support the child and enhance his or her well-being and self-esteem.

Dr Glenys Jones
Chartered Psychologist
Autism Centre for Education and Research
University of Birmingham

Introduction for adults

This book has been written to help both children and adults understand what it's like to have autism. It is written in two "voices" – Tom's and mine. The words in the first section are written as if spoken by Tom, as if he is telling you about his autism. The second part of the book is written in my adult voice, for adults: it gives information, and suggests ideas and strategies that can help a child with autism.

Since you are reading this book, you probably know someone with autism, and probably realise that a young child with autism would not have the insights into autism that Tom expresses, or use language in the way Tom does. Unlike Tom, you probably have the ability to think flexibly, use your imagination and knowingly "suspend disbelief". So I would ask you to do just that – and listen to the words that Tom might tell you if he could.

I would also ask you to point out to any children reading this book that Tom wouldn't really use words in the way he does in this book. Please suggest that they start by reading the "Introduction for children" on the next page.

Autism is caused by differences in the way the brain develops, and although it is a lifelong condition, it changes over time. With the right support, many people with autism can improve their communication skills and come to enjoy friendships – whether they are "able" or whether they have what's sometimes called "classic autism", with its associated learning difficulties. There's no one-size-fits-all way to help, but I hope that an understanding of some of the ideas and strategies in this book will help you to help the children you know.

Introduction for children

Meet Tom – a young boy with autism.

Tom will tell you what it feels like to have autism. He'll tell you what he likes and what he doesn't like. He'll tell you things that make life easier or more difficult for him – and the ways in which other people might help him.

A child with autism would not usually talk in the way Tom does – but these are the sorts of things Tom might tell you if he could.

"I'd like to tell you how autism makes me feel, and the things that help me."

"You may not see straight away that I have autism. I look like most other boys. But having autism can affect how I behave and talk in some situations. Autism affects each person differently. So other children with autism may be like me in lots of ways, but are not exactly the same as me.

I have problems in making sense of the world around me, especially making sense of what other people say and do. It's very hard for me to imagine what other children and adults might be thinking or feeling, or know what they intend to do. That's why I find it difficult to communicate and play with them.

I also have big difficulties coping with change. If things stay the same I know what to expect, but when things change, I don't know what will happen, and I get anxious. If I'm anxious I might not be able to tell you with words, but I may show it by getting very upset, and might cry or hit out or run away.

I have problems with 'sensory' things like sounds and lights and touch and smells. Loud noises, the smell of some foods and flickering lights are difficult for me to cope with.

Like lots of children with autism, I also have some problems with learning to read and write and with answering teachers' questions in class."

"Most children seem to know what others are feeling and thinking, and get along together easily. I can't see how they do that."

"You might not realise it, but most people just naturally 'pick up' what other people are thinking or feeling. This helps them make sense of each other and 'tune in' to one another.

We are taught that our senses are sight, hearing, taste, touch and smell. But there is another sense – which has been called the 'social sense'. Just like someone who is blind has problems with their sight, I have problems with this 'social sense'. Some people have said that autism is a kind of 'social blindness' or 'mind blindness', because having autism makes it difficult to 'read' what's going on in other people's minds.

Most people can work out (without even trying to) what other people are thinking or feeling or intending to do from the words they use, the expressions on their face, their tone of voice, their gestures and body movements. It's as if they can read messages in each other's eyes – as if they can see and share their invisible thoughts and feelings. But I can't do that. Because of my 'mind blindness', people seem unpredictable, and I find the world very confusing."

"If I have to look at someone while I'm
listening to them, I feel overloaded
by lots of information. When Mum
reads to me, I like it better if I'm
facing the same way as her."

"Most people look at each other when they are listening and talking. But I feel uncomfortable looking at people, and I usually don't. If I have to look at someone while I listen, I can feel overwhelmed by all the information coming in through my ears and eyes. I listen better when I'm not looking at the person who's talking. So it can appear as if I'm not listening even when I am.

Mum and Dad used to think I was deaf, because I often took no notice when they spoke to me. Sometimes I get so fixed on playing with something that I can't hear other people talking to me.

If you want to get my attention, it helps to say my name first – at the beginning of the sentence. Like 'Tom – put your coat on, please.' If you say 'Put your coat on please, Tom,' I might not even notice you're talking until I hear my name.

When most people listen to other people, they naturally make sense of that person's 'tone of voice'. But I can't interpret 'tone of voice', and usually can't tell if someone is talking in a friendly way or being sarcastic or annoyed.

I also find it difficult to understand people if they don't say exactly what they mean. I understand things in a 'literal' way. When my teacher told us to paint the child next us, I thought she meant to put paint on that person. When she said school was breaking up, I got very frightened, because I thought the school building was going to break into pieces."

"I often copy words I hear. People call me 'you' when they're talking to me. I copy that, and call myself 'you' too."

"I didn't start talking until I was about three years old, which is later than most children. I do say words and phrases now, but I don't chat, or talk about my day, or make up stories the way my little brother does. When I do talk I sometimes repeat what I hear other people say.*

Even though I don't talk very much, my parents and teachers are helping me to learn to use words to communicate. They use words to comment on what I'm doing, and encourage me to use words myself to ask for what I want and to make choices using pictures linked with written words. That helps me to learn to ask for things and talk about things.

Sometimes I use words when I'm being read to. I've heard my favourite stories so often I know them off by heart. When Mum or the teacher makes a mistake, I don't like it, and tell them what it should be. Sometimes Mum leaves out a word and pauses – then I say it! When I was younger, we used to play a game where Mum sang nursery rhymes, but left a gap. So she would sing 'Twinkle, twinkle...', and I would sing 'little star'."

---

* *Echolalia* – the repetition, or echoing, of words or phrases is common in autism. It leads to pronoun reversal: the child hears himself referred to as "you", as in "Do you want a biscuit?", and he repeats this, saying, "Do you want a biscuit?" or "You want a biscuit", meaning "I want a biscuit".

"I have difficulty understanding facial expressions and using gestures to communicate. If I want something out of reach, instead of pointing to it, I might take someone's hand and lead them to it."

"Language isn't just the words people use. People's 'body language' can show how they feel or what they think or what they intend to do. People use gestures – like waving and pointing. And without even being aware of it, their posture and expressions change, depending on what they're thinking and feeling. Most people – even toddlers – naturally know how to interpret body language and the expressions on people's faces. But I don't.

People's faces move and change, but I can't understand why. Their mouth turns up in a smile, their eyebrows move, or they crease their nose up, but I don't know what those things mean. It might be obvious to you that someone looks bored or suspicious or disappointed – but I can't 'read' different expressions the way most people can. I can be helped to learn.* You might also notice that my face doesn't show the range of expressions you see on other children's faces.

Gestures are also difficult for me to understand and use. Mum and Dad encourage me to communicate about things I want or like by teaching me to point."

---

* See page 59 for information on a resource designed to help people with autism interpret body language.

"Other children have fun playing
with each other. I usually play with
things, not other children."

"I don't usually find it fun playing with other children, because I'm not sure what to do or how to join in. I sometimes play alongside other children, but not usually *with* them.

Other children just seem to get on with each other, chatting and laughing and sharing make-believe games or taking it in turns to do things. But I can't work out what other children are thinking or feeling, or intending to do, so I just find all that very confusing.

I usually play with things rather than people. I like to spin the wheels of my Thomas the Tank Engines. I hold the wheels up close to my face and look out of the corner of my eyes. I also like lining up my engines, sorting my LEGO® into different colours, building LEGO® models, and watching my favourite Thomas DVDs.

I like bouncing on the trampoline and sometimes I enjoy rough-and-tumble play with Dad. And I enjoy being pushed on the swings. Bouncing, rocking and swinging usually make me feel calm. But when we're in the park, I will only go on the swings if I can go on the special swing I always go on. If someone else is using it, I get upset."

"I like repeating things. Like drawing trains. I draw lots of pictures of trains. It makes me feel calm."

"I find the world a confusing, unpredictable place. So I try to get some sense of order by having routines that don't change. That helps me feel reassured and calm, because I know what will happen next. Otherwise I get very scared and stressed.

It's important to me that things happen in the same way as they usually do and in a certain order – things like being picked up at our gate by the school bus, sitting in my usual seat, and going our usual route to school. If it's a different driver from usual, or if we suddenly have to go a different way, I can get very upset.

I like to repeat things. I spin around and around, and walk back and forth. I look at the same books and watch the same DVDs over and over. I like to keep flicking paper and looking at it. I draw lots of pictures of trains.

Having routines and repeating things helps me relax. It helps me know what is going to happen next. I can get very upset if things change unexpectedly from the way they usually happen. But I *can* cope with change better if someone prepares me."

"Mum makes a visual timetable to show me what will happen. My teacher makes one for me too, and we look at it together."

"Lots of people can cope with changes in routine and plans, and enjoy surprises. But change and surprises make me VERY anxious. When I'm anxious I might cry or scream or run away.

Most children like surprise presents on their birthday, but I don't. I like to know what I'm going to get on my birthday, so I'm prepared for it and it's not a shock. Mum and Dad show me my presents before they wrap them up.

Because I don't like change or surprises, I feel calmer if I know what is going to happen – at home, and at school. It helps to have a visual timetable* that shows me what to expect. Mum makes a visual timetable for the day and the week – and my teacher uses one to show what's going to happen at school. That makes me feel safe and secure. When I feel safe I behave more calmly.

If there's going to be a change to my routine, it doesn't feel so scary if I can *see* that change coming – on my visual timetable. It also helps if Mum or my teacher writes me a Social Story™** about something new that is going to happen.

I also need to be prepared for changing from one activity or place to another. As well as having a visual timetable, it helps if I'm told and shown that it's almost time to stop or change what I'm doing. Near the end of a swimming lesson, my teacher holds up a countdown clock, tells me when it's 10 minutes to go, then when it's 5 minutes to go , and when it's time to stop, he counts 5, 4, 3, 2, 1...and out!"

---

*   For information on visual timetables, see pages 41 and 42.
** For information on Social Stories™, see page 42.

"I don't pick up 'social rules' the way most children do, so I need to be taught what things like 'standing too close' mean."

"Unless I'm told, I don't know if I'm behaving in a way I'm not supposed to, or saying things that are not polite. Other children usually 'pick up' how they are supposed to behave in different situations. But because I have autism, I need to be taught exactly what's OK and what's not OK in different places and with different people.

I used to sit 'too close' to people and go up to people and put my face right next to theirs. I wasn't meaning to be rude. I had no idea that you weren't supposed to do that, and I didn't know what 'too close' meant. Mum and Dad used drawings and a Social Story™ to help me understand, and taught me the 'arm's length' rule (keep about an arm's length away from people or it's too close for comfort).

There are lots of 'social rules' that are obvious to most children, but are not obvious to me, so I need to be taught them. Until my Mum and Dad taught me, I didn't realise that some games had a 'winner' and a 'loser', for example. Some children with autism might ask grown-ups questions like 'How old are you?', or say 'You're fat' – not because they are being deliberately rude or naughty, but because they haven't been taught that it's not OK to do that."

"When I'm somewhere noisy,
it hurts my ears."

"Not everyone with autism has the same sensory problems, but most are unusually sensitive – in different ways – to things they see, hear, touch, taste or smell.

With some things, like sounds, lights and smells, I'm over-sensitive. Sounds and sights that most people aren't even aware of can upset me. I can't filter out background noise, so even a ticking clock can sound loud and distracting. Loud noises like vacuum cleaners are scary and painful. I feel overwhelmed and panicky in noisy places with bright, flickering lights. I feel ill if I smell certain foods or perfume.

I sometimes wear headphones to block outside noises. I'm scared to go into public toilets because of noisy hand dryers. I don't enjoy birthday parties, especially if there are balloons, because I think they might burst and make a loud noise. I really don't like fireworks. And even though I enjoy going to the swimming pool, I have to go when it's quiet. When lots of children are there shouting and playing, the noise hurts and I have to put my hands over my ears.

With touch, it's the opposite for me. I need a heavy blanket on my bed to get me settled, or I don't feel I'm covered. But other children with autism might be over-sensitive to touch. Some can't bear the touch of rough clothes or labels. Some find a light touch painful, but are fine with a tight hug."

"Even though I found it difficult to learn to ride my bike, I can do it now! My little brother and I ride around the park sometimes."

"I have some problems with 'motor' skills, which means I can't always coordinate my body movements. Some things that involve big movements, like playing catch, walking on uneven surfaces, running and playing football are difficult. (Football seems impossible anyway, because I never know what I'm supposed to do, and everything happens so fast and is so confusing).

It was hard learning to ride a bike, because balancing and making my legs and arms work together was a real problem. But Mum and Dad spent ages teaching me, and now I can do it! It feels great, and Mum and Dad are very proud of me. I'm learning to swim too, and really enjoy it.

It's also tricky for me to do some fiddly tasks with my hands – things like using scissors, doing up buttons, and doing up shoe laces. Mum is still teaching me, by breaking down the job into little steps, and using a special lacing board.

Not all children with autism have the same problems as me – some are very good at doing fiddly tasks with their hands. And I'm OK with some things, like using a pencil for drawing, and building my LEGO®."

"To encourage me to eat, Mum and Dad got me a Thomas the Tank Engine plate, so when I eat, I get to see the picture."

"Everyone's daily life includes eating and sleeping. Most people take these basic things for granted, but they have been real problems for me – and my family.

Take eating. Mum and Dad try lots of ways to help me eat different things, but I can't stand the smell or texture of some foods, and I won't eat sandwiches or a meal with 'bits' mixed up in it.

At school, I couldn't eat because the lunch hall was too busy and noisy. So now I eat my lunch in a quiet area next to the main lunch hall, with a few other children.

Like a lot of children with autism, I've had problems with my tummy, and sometimes I get tummy pains. Mum took me to the doctor about it.

Sleep has been a problem too. I used to take a REALLY long time to fall asleep. Now Mum or Dad reads me a Social Story™ about sleeping at bedtime, makes my room dark with blackout blinds, gives me a foot massage, and puts a weighted blanket* on my bed to help me get settled. These things have helped a lot, but I still have trouble sometimes."

---

* See page 39 for information on the safe use of weighted blankets and vests.

"I go to LEGO® Club with other children who have autism. We are learning to work together to build things. It's fun!"

"Most children with autism have 'special interests', things they really, really like. My favourite things are Thomas the Tank Engine, other trains, wheels, and LEGO®. I like singing too.

I like to line up my trains, and look at them, or watch the wheels as they spin. I like to watch my Thomas DVDs and sing along with the songs. People say I have a lovely voice and always get the notes right.

I also like drawing trains, sorting my LEGO® and building things with the blocks. When I'm doing something with trains or LEGO®, I feel calm and happy. If someone suddenly makes me stop, without preparing me, I can get very upset.

Sometimes my teachers use my special interest as a reward. If I finish my work, I can play with Thomas for five minutes. They put a picture of Thomas on my visual timetable, so I know it's coming. My visual timetable also helps me see that it's not always time to play with Thomas.

Lots of children with autism like LEGO®, so Mum and Dad take me to a LEGO® club at the weekend. I have fun. As we build things together, I'm learning to play in a group of friends."

How adults can help

Parents and teachers need to work together to provide the consistency that children with autism desperately need. Whether they are at home, at school or out and about, they experience the world as a confusing, unpredictable place. We can help in many ways, including by:

- creating a sense of STRUCTURE

- PREPARING for change (remember the 3 Ps: Preparation Prevents Panic)

- recognising that people with autism are often "visual thinkers", and can be greatly helped with VISUAL supports such as pictures, photos and the written word

- remembering that people with autism are literal thinkers, and are likely to take the words you say LITERALLY. So be aware of language that could be misinterpreted. Try to be accurate and precise in your choice of words. Be aware that ambiguous language, metaphors, jokes and sarcasm can confuse and distress a child with autism

- being aware of SENSORY issues, and adapting accordingly, for example:

  - if necessary, giving the child headphones to block out unwanted noise

- not wearing perfume if the smell upsets the child

- cutting out the labels in clothes if they upset the child who is hyper-sensitive to touch

- perhaps trying a "weighted vest" or "weighted blanket" to comfort and settle someone if they are hyposensitive to touch. The extra weight can provide "proprioceptive feedback" (body awareness) and help them to feel settled and calm. For safety reasons, weighted blankets should be used with caution. It is wise to obtain advice from a health professional to make sure that a weighted blanket is suitable, and to ensure that the weight of the blanket is appropriate for the child's size and weight. It's important to make sure that the child's head cannot be covered by the blanket and that the child can easily remove the blanket if he or she wishes. It is recommended that the child should never be left unattended when using a weighted blanket, and some sources also recommend a time limit

- keeping STRESS and AROUSAL levels as LOW as possible by keeping the environment CALM and ORDERED

- helping the child make sense of their world, by providing them with MEANINGFUL INFORMATION in a way that they can understand. Social Stories™ and Comic Strip Conversations are key techniques (see 42–45)

- teaching the child how to work and play successfully with others – trying to find an activity that the child with autism can do as well as or better than the other children

- making sure everyone working with the child understands their needs. It is very helpful to write a personal "passport" or "profile" to share with people who do not know the child, setting out the child's skills and interests and the activities he enjoys, and giving information on how he communicates, any sensory issues he has, what upsets him, what comforts him when he is upset, and any issues around eating, toileting and changes to routine. On page 64 is a template that you can fill in if you have a child in your family or in your school with autism. It might be helpful to use it with this book, so that you can share information about autism in general, and about that child in particular.

MAKE IT VISUAL!

In our everyday life, we all benefit from visual supports, from road signs to maps to toilet signs to calendars, which help us navigate our way through life. Visual supports are especially important to people (adults as well as children) on the autism spectrum, because many "think in pictures". Photos and pictures are essential if the person cannot read.

Visual supports can provide information and structure, aid communication, prepare for change, provide reassurance, reduce anxiety and help the child make sense of the world.

Visual supports – which are most effective when they are tailored to a particular child's needs and interests – can be used for many things, and in many ways, including:

- teaching life skills, e.g. using drawings or photos to show the sequence necessary for brushing your teeth, using the loo and washing your hands

- using pictures to encourage and enable the child to choose between one activity/drink/whatever, and another

- using a visual timetable to show the sequence of what will happen that day. Attaching images with velcro allows a sequence of images to be made, and changed as necessary. (The number of written words they contain will depend on the needs and abilities of the child)

- rewarding and encouraging appropriate behaviour, with star charts linked to their favourite activity, etc.

- using auditory and visual prompts such as timers/clocks to indicate the start and finish for activities

- showing levels/scales of mood or anxiety in a visual way. Creating a picture of a "mood thermometer" can help the child become more aware of changes in levels of anxiety or happiness, and enable him to communicate these

- using systems such as the PECS (Picture Exchange Communication System) to aid communication through the use of pictures and symbols

- using colour-coded school decor to help provide clear structure in the environment

- using colour-coded files to help organise work into subject areas and/or prioritise tasks

- using illustrated Social Stories™ to teach a skill or concept, prepare for an activity or change, and celebrate success, etc.

- using Comic Strip Conversations to explore social interactions

- ...the list is virtually ENDLESS. (Note that using CAPITALS is a visual way of indicating importance).

See the National Autistic Society website www.autism.org.uk for a detailed information sheet on visual supports, including visual timetables, and how to use them. It includes links to useful websites. You can use this link: www.autism.org.uk/living-with-autism/strategies-and-approaches/visual-supports.aspx

SOCIAL STORIES™

As Tom has told you, someone with autism has difficulty making sense of the social world. Gaps in social understanding can easily lead to increased, stress, frustration and inappropriate behaviour. A key way of filling in the gaps in social understanding is to use Social Stories™.

This strategy was first developed in the USA by Carol Gray, when she was working in schools with children with autism and Asperger Syndrome. Since the 1990s, when the technique was devised, it has become part of "good practice" worldwide. Parents, teachers and other professionals can use Social Stories™, and research has shown the technique to be very effective in improving social understanding – and, consequently, social behaviour.

Social Stories™ are remarkably flexible, as they can be tailored to suit any child and any situation. They help the child make sense of social situations in terms of what happens, what's expected, who does what, where, when, why, etc., and how other people might feel.

In Carol Gray's words, "A Social Story™ describes a situation, skill, or concept in terms of relevant social cues, perspectives, and common responses in a specifically defined style and format. The goal of a Social Story™ is to share accurate social information in a patient and reassuring manner that is easily understood by its audience."

Social Stories™ can be used to:

- applaud and celebrate achievements and successful behaviour – so that the child knows when he has "done well". For example, Tom's parents could write him a Social Story™ celebrating him trying hard and learning to ride his bike

- prepare for upcoming events or change, so that the child can be reassured by knowing what is going to happen. For example, Tom's teacher could write a Social Story™ about the fact that a new assistant will be joining the class

- reveal "the hidden social code" – provide the social information which most children pick up naturally, but which children with autism do not. Helping the child to understand the expectations of the social world enables him to learn new skills, develop appropriate behaviour, and reduce unwanted behaviour. For example, on page 29, you may remember that Tom's parents wrote a Social Story™ to introduce him to the concept of standing "too close" to someone, to explain how that makes other people feel, and to guide Tom to stand at an appropriate/ comfortable distance ("arm's length away") from people.

You may have noticed the ™ (trademark) sign every time the term Social Stories™ is written, and may wonder how Social Stories™ differ from any "social story" written to explain something 'social' to a child? Social Stories™ involve a very specific way of writing (with or without illustrations) according to guidelines Carol Gray has developed and fine-tuned over the years.

It takes time, training and perseverance to write a positive, patient, effective Social Story™, but it is worth it. It's important to stick to the guidelines to avoid pitfalls. A possible pitfall is to see Social Stories™ as tools for providing a "quick fix" for "problem" behaviour, and if you're not careful, you might find that you've slipped into negative language. That is likely to add to a child's stress rather than decrease it. So it is very important to make sure you follow Gray's guidelines (see references on the next page), and check what you have written against Gray's Social Story™ checklist before you read the Social Story™ with your child.

I'm a great fan of Social Stories™, not only because they help the child to understand the world, but because they help us to understand the child. Preparing to write them involves gathering information and *taking time to consider the situation from the child's point of view*. This conscious, careful taking of the child's perspective undoubtedly increases *our* understanding and appreciation of what the world is like for a child with autism. That increased understanding can alter attitudes, and increase empathy and compassion.

For information on Social Stories™ and how to write them, see www.carolgraysocialstories.com, www.thegraycenter.org and/or Carol Gray (2010) *The New Social Story Book*. (Arlington, TX: Future Horizons Inc.) Also see Marie Howley and Eileen Arnold, with a foreword by Carol Gray (2005) *Revealing the Hidden Social Code: Social Stories™ for People with Autistic Spectrum Disorder*. (London: Jessica Kingsley Publishers.)

COMIC STRIP CONVERSATIONS

Another very useful technique developed by Carol Gray is the "Comic Strip Conversation". Inspired by the evidence that visual supports aid learning, this technique involves drawing cartoon figures (amateurish stick figures are fine!) with speech bubbles and thought bubbles to help the child identify what people might be thinking, as well as what they might say/have said in a social situation. For more detail, see www.thegraycenter.org and Carol Gray (1994) *Comic Strip Conversations*. (Arlington, TX: Future Horizons Inc.)

COPING WITH TOILETING ISSUES

I omitted this from Tom's section, because I'm aware that if children read that a classmate of theirs might have toileting problems, it could unfortunately lead to teasing rather than compassion. However, it's a common problem, which needs to be included in this book.

Toileting issues can be very distressing for the child and the family. Children with autism are often late to stop using nappies (some may never do so), and many resist using a toilet. Some may avoid opening their bowels for days at a time, and suffer severe tummy pains and stress.

Parents may need to seek expert help from their doctor and other autism professionals.

Sometimes there are problems with proprioception (body awareness), and the brain may not recognise the body's signals. Sometimes, fear of the toilet is the underlying cause, and there are various techniques to help the child to get over this. The child may not understand what's happening, and may think his insides will fall out, or be afraid of the sound of splashing water. Establishing a calm toileting routine and gradually transitioning from nappy to potty or loo may help. A Social Story™ may help reassure the child that it is safe to use the loo.

"CHALLENGING" BEHAVIOUR

Having autism can make life very stressful, and stress can show itself in a variety of ways. It may help to remember that what is sometimes referred to as "challenging" behaviour in a child with autism could be better described as "distressed behaviour".

Using some of the strategies outlined earlier to create structure, aid understanding and prepare for change can help reduce the child's stress, and so reduce the likelihood of outbursts, meltdowns and tantrums. However, we live in a less-than-perfect world: stress levels may rise, and meltdowns may ensue.

School is often a stressful place for a child with autism. Many parents recognise a "Jeckyll and Hyde" aspect – when their child is "well behaved" at school, but has a meltdown on their return home, or vice versa. This can be the consequence of a build-up of stress upon stress (too much noise, a change of plan, a new teacher, etc.) throughout the school day, so that the child "explodes" at school, or when they reach the security of home.

Dealing with meltdowns is never easy, but it can help to keep in mind the mantra "LOW AND SLOW". Aim to lower the child's stress and arousal levels. Don't try to impose eye contact. Keep your movements slow. Speak "low" (quietly), and slow, and use only a few, simple words. Or say nothing at all if speech increases their stress levels. Don't raise your voice.

Perhaps try showing a visual support card with a soothing image or a couple of words that your child understands – such as IT'S OK. STAY CALM. Avoid joining in or engaging in conversation that could escalate the distress, and try not to take anything your child says personally. Allow your child the time and space to calm down.

Remember that a child's parents are the experts on that child. So if you as a parent find a particular thing or sequence that works to help calm *your* child down, or prevents your child getting over-stressed in the first place, write it down and pass it on to family, friends and teachers. That way, they can follow your lead and provide the child with a loving, consistent, structured approach that will help make their world a less stressful and confusing place to live.

More about autism

THE VOCABULARY OF AUTISM
– JARGON BUSTER

If the world of autism is new to you, as it would be if a child has recently been diagnosed, the language used when parents and professionals discuss autism can be rather bewildering at first. This section introduces you to a few of the significant terms you might come across – not in A–Z order, but (rather vaguely!) in order of significance/the order you might become aware of them.

The triad of impairments

At the point of diagnosis, or shortly after, you may hear people talking about "the triad" – meaning the "triad of impairments". This term was first used by Dr Lorna Wing to describe three key areas of difficulty that are the hallmarks of autism:

1. social interaction

2. social communication

3. social imagination.

The third part of the triad was later changed by some professionals from "imagination" to "flexibility in thinking and behaviour" – reflecting the fact that the impairment involves *social imagination*, thinking flexibly enough to play imaginatively and imagine what other people might be thinking or feeling.

Many experts see the first two aspects of the triad being inextricably linked – and the current view is to consider the key elements of autism as:

- problems with social communication and interaction

- restricted, repetitive patterns of behaviour, interests and activities.

It has also been recognised that many children with autism have sensory issues too, in that they may be over- or under-sensitive to sounds, sights, taste, touch and smell, and have delayed and fragmented perception.

- Perception may be delayed in that it may take longer than usual to process incoming information. This leads to problems with many things, from understanding what's being said to coping with rapidly changing situations such as social and sporting activities.

- Fragmented perception means perceiving things as disconnected fragments, and not being able to process those fragments into a meaningful whole. So someone with autism might perceive a nose, a mouth and eyes as fragments – rather than perceiving a face as a coherent whole. They might not recognise someone wearing unfamiliar clothes. They might hear a few words rather than a whole sentence.

The autism spectrum

People often refer to someone with autism as "being on the spectrum" – meaning the "autism spectrum". Autism is described as a spectrum condition, because although everyone with autism shares key difficulties with social communication and interaction, and with thinking and behaving flexibly, the exact pattern of difficulties and the level of severity varies. Some people with autism have learning disability, and some do not. Some are less rigid in their thinking than others, some have more (and different) problems with sensory and motor issues than others, and so on.

ASC or ASD? Condition or disorder?

Although the term Autism Spectrum Disorder (ASD) is the most commonly used term, many prefer to use the term Autism Spectrum Condition (ASC), because it has less negative connotations . Increasingly, just the phrase "autism spectrum" is being used.

High Functioning Autism or Asperger Syndrome?

Autism can occur with all levels of intelligence. Individuals with "classic" autism typically have learning difficulties (a below-average IQ). Individuals with autism who have an average or above-average IQ may have been diagnosed as having High Functioning Autism (HFA) or able autism or Asperger Syndrome (AS). There is still debate about whether HFA or able autism is in fact the same condition as AS.

Some experts have distinguished between the two:

- diagnosing HFA or able autism if the person has the key difficulties of autism, an average or above-average IQ, but had delayed language development

- diagnosing Asperger Syndrome if the person has the key difficulties of autism, an average or above-average IQ, and no delay in language development.

The debate about this distinction is likely to continue. A significant and controversial change to the diagnostic criteria occurred when the (fifth) edition of the influential *Diagnostic and Statistical Manual of the American Psychiatric Association* (known as DSM-5) was published in May 2013. In DSM-5, the diagnosis of "Asperger Syndrome", which had first been included in the previous edition of the manual (DSM-4, published in 1994) was *removed* as a separate subgroup. One of the aims of DSM-5 was to remove all subgroups and have a sliding scale for a single diagnosis of Autism Spectrum Disorder: Asperger Syndrome was absorbed within this overall diagnosis.

DSM-5 is an American publication, and there are other sets of criteria used for making a diagnosis, so it's not yet clear what the implications of this change will be worldwide. It seems likely that terms such as High Functioning Autism, able autism and Asperger Syndrome will continue to be used among members of the autism community.

Neurotypical (NT)

The term "neurotypical" – often shortened to NT – is sometimes used to describe someone with a "typical" brain, as opposed to someone with autism. The brains of people with autism develop differently from neurotypical brains, and it is these brain differences that underlie autism.

CF/GF

"The CF/GF diet" stands for "casein-free/gluten-free diet". Some parents try eliminating casein (a protein found in dairy foods) and/or gluten (a protein found in wheat, barley, rye and oats) from their child's diet. There have been anecdotal reports that this can help some children with a range of issues from digestive problems to attention, communication and sleep. However, anecdotal evidence about the effectiveness of the CF/GF diet is mixed and scientific evidence is weak. Since restricted diets run the risk of leading to malnutrition, they should be carried out with care, after referring to a doctor. For more details, see *A Brief Guide to Autism Treatments* by Elisabeth Hollister Sandberg and Becky L. Spritz (2013, Jessica Kinglsey Publishers) pp.79–87.

Savant

"Savant" comes from the French *savoir*, to know, and refers to someone with an area of exceptional ability. Following the release of the 1988 film *Rain Man*, in which Dustin Hoffmann plays a character with autism who has savant ability with numbers, many people came to think that savant abilities were common among people with autism. However, this is not the case – it is thought that less than one per cent of people with autism has savant abilities.

The following are some terms you may hear when discussing the many sensory issues involved in autism:

Hypo – Meaning hyposensitive, or under-sensitive.

Hyper – Meaning hypersensitive, or over-sensitive.

Vestibular system – Our vestibular system, situated in our inner ear, helps us maintain our balance and tells us how fast our bodies are moving. People with autism may have hypo- or hypersensitive vestibular systems. The need to rock or swing or spin may be a sign of a *hypo*sensitive vestibular system.

Car sickness and difficulties with sporting activities that involve controlling body movements or stopping quickly may be linked to a *hyper*sensitive vestibular system.

Proprioception – Proprioception is our "body awareness" system, which integrates information about the position and movement of our bodies in space. People with autism may have hypo- or hypersensitive proprioceptive systems, which can lead to problems such as standing "too close" to people, bumping into things, the need to lean on desks or wear hats to feel where their bodies are, and to difficulties with "fine" motor skills such as doing up buttons and using scissors.

Synaesthesia – This is a rare form of sensory perception which affects some people on the autism spectrum. A person with synaesthesia experiences a sensation in one sensory system (such as hearing) but perceives that sensation in another (such as sight). So they might hear a sound, or smell a particular aroma and see it as a colour.

ANSWERING QUESTIONS ABOUT AUTISM

In this section, some of the basic questions about autism are answered.

When was autism first recognised as a condition?

In the 1940s, American child psychiatrist Dr Leo Kanner first described "early infantile autism" in a group of learning-disabled children with whom he was working. The word "autism" comes from the Greek "autos", meaning self – reflecting the fact that these children were socially isolated, by themselves, removed from interaction with others. "Classic autism" is sometimes referred to as "Kanner's autism".

Around the same time, the Viennese paediatrician Dr Hans Asperger was working in Vienna with another unusual group of children, who didn't have learning disabilities, whom he described as "autistic". Asperger wrote in German, and his work was largely ignored in the English-speaking world until 1981, when the term "Asperger Syndrome" was first used in an article by psychiatrist Dr Lorna Wing.

One of the founding parents of the National Autistic Society, whose daughter had classic autism, Lorna Wing argued that autism was a spectrum condition, and used the term Asperger Syndrome to describe a subgroup of children with whom she had been working.

What causes autism?

Many years ago, in the 1960s, some experts used to think that autism was a result of cold or inappropriate parenting. This theory has been shown to be WRONG! Autism is caused by unusual brain development, which particularly affects the parts of the brain that process social information.

No-one is sure exactly what causes the brain to develop differently from a "neurotypical" brain, but research suggests it is a combination of genetic and environmental factors. Related conditions such as dyslexia (see the next page) are more likely to be found in other family members, and close relatives may have "echoes" of some of the characteristics of autism even if they do not have autism itself.

How common is autism?

- Roughly one per cent of the population is on the autism spectrum.

- The ratio of boys to girls is 4:1.

- If one child in the family has autism, there is thought to be a 5–10 per cent chance of a sibling (brother or sister) having autism too.

Can autism occur with other conditions?

- Autism can occur with or without any other physical, psychological condition or learning disability.

- Related/overlapping conditions include:

  - **Dyspraxia** (aka Developmental Coordination Disorder) – a condition affecting the way the brain processes information involved in planning and organisation – particularly of movement.

  - **ADHD** (Attention Deficit Hyperactivity Disorder) – characterised by problems with attention, impulsivity and hyperactivity.

  - **PDA** (Pathological Demand Avoidance Syndrome) – increasingly recognised as being part of the autism spectrum, PDA is characterised by resistance to the ordinary, everyday demands of life.

  - **Dyslexia** – a condition affecting the development of reading, writing and other language-related skills.

- Children with autism are more likely than most children to develop epilepsy at some time in their childhood and adolescence.

- More about these conditions can be found in individual titles in the *Can I tell you about...?* series.

How do you explain the difficulties experienced by someone with autism?

There are a number of theories about the underlying psychology of autism:

- **Theory of Mind.** People with autism have difficulty with what is known as theory of mind (ToM) or "mind reading". They have great problems "putting themselves in someone else's shoes" or imagining what other people think or feel or intend to do. This is sometimes referred to as "mind blindness".

- **Weak central coherence**. Although they may have great skills in attending to detail, people with autism have difficulty integrating details into a whole. In order to make sense of experience, the brain needs to piece together fragmented details in order to see "the bigger picture". Someone with autism can find that difficult.

- **Executive function.** The brains of people with autism have problems with what is known as "executive function": they have difficulty planning and organising, and in switching their attention from one thing to another.

- **Monotropism.** This theory was developed by psychologist Dr Wendy Lawson, who has Asperger Syndrome. People with autism can only focus on one thing at a time, which they do with intensity. They have difficulty multi-tasking or holding their focus on more than one thing at a time.

- **Empathising/systemising (E-S) theory**. According to this theory, developed by Professor Simon Baron-Cohen, all people can be classified according to their "scores" as empathisers (who are driven to identify and respond appropriately to other people's feelings) and systematisers (who are driven to construct systems and identify patterns and rules). People with autism show low empathising skills, but high systematising skills.

  This may explain such characteristics as repeated behaviours, narrow interests and routines, which may be seen as a systematic search for predictable rules. The E-S theory is linked to Simon Baron-Cohen's "extreme male brain" theory of autism. Baron-Cohen's research has found that in the general population, males tend to score more highly than females as systematisers, while females score more highly as empathisers. Since people with autism score highly as systematisers, this may explain why there are significantly more males than females with autism.

Recommended reading, resources, websites and organisations

BOOKS

Christie, P., Newson, E., Prevezer, W. and Chandler, S. (2009) *First Steps in Intervention with your Child with Autism: Frameworks for Communication*. London: Jessica Kingsley Publishers.

A beautifully written and sensitively illustrated book, with strategies for encouraging social communication and interactive play.

Howley, M. and Arnold, E., with a foreword by Carol Gray (2005) *Revealing the Hidden Social Code: Social Stories™ for People with Autistic Spectrum Disorder*. London: Jessica Kingsley Publishers.

A great resource, packed with illustrated examples of Social Stories™ and clear information about how to go about writing them.

Hollister Sandberg, E. and Spritz, B.L. (2013) *A Brief Guide to Autism Treatments*. London: Jessica Kingsley Publishers.

This concise guide helps parents to understand and evaluate the sometimes bewildering array of therapeutic interventions available.

DVDS AND CD-ROMS

A is for Autism (1992)

This short film uses voice, drawings and animation. Created from contributions by people with autism, it provides a vivid insight into their experience.

The Autism Puzzle (2002–3)

Downloadable from the internet for free, this fascinating documentary was made for the BBC by Saskia Baron, inspired by her brother, who has autism. It explores the history of autism, shows a range of different children and adults with autism, and examines research into what causes autism and how people with autism perceive the world.

Mind Reading: The Interactive Guide to Emotions. Simon
Baron-Cohen. London: Jessica Kingsley Publishers.

This unique interactive resource uses games and quizzes to help
improve the recognition of emotions. Video clips and audio clips
illustrate the way facial expressions, body language and tone of voice
express emotions. It is available as a DVD-ROM and also as a set of
CD-ROMs.

WEBSITES

www.autismeducationtrust.org.uk

Launched in 2007 with government funding, the Autism Education
Trust is an umbrella organisation that supports and promotes good
education practice for all children and young people on the autism
spectrum in England. The website includes a multitude of useful
resources. For information on how to support a child with autism,
click on the Inclusion Development Programme, and follow the links
to the Autism modules. For ideas on "What makes an effective school
for children with autism", click on National Standards. For ideas on
"What makes an effective practitioner for a child with autism", click
on Competency Framework.

www.carolgraysocialstories.com

A new website with information on Carol Gray's Social Stories™.
This website has a link to The Gray Center for Social Learning
and Understanding (www.thegraycenter.org), which is a non-profit
organisation that "cultivates the strengths of individuals with
autism and those who interact with them, and globally promotes
social understanding".

www.researchautism.net

Research Autism is a UK charity dedicated to research into
interventions in autism. They carry out independent research into
new and existing health, education, social and other interventions

www.autismresearchcentre.com

Based in the University of Cambridge, UK, the Autism Research
Centre aims to understand the biomedical causes of autism
spectrum conditions, and develop new methods for assessment and
intervention. You can access many research papers on its website,
including one on LEGO® therapy.

NATIONAL AND INTERNATIONAL ORGANISATIONS

UK
The National Autistic Society
393 City Road
London
EC1V 1NG
Phone: +44 (0)20 7833 2299
Email: nas@nas.org.uk
Website: www.autism.org.uk

Northern Ireland
Autism NI
Donard House
Knockbracken Healthcare Park
Saintfield Road
Belfast
BT8 8BH
Phone: +44 (0)28 90 401729
Helpline: 0845 055 9010
Email: info@autismni.org
Website: www.autismni.org

The National Autistic Society Northern Ireland
59 Malone Road
Belfast
BT9 6SA
Phone: +44 (0) 28 90 687066
Email: northernireland@nas.org.uk
Website: www.autism.org.uk/northernireland

Scotland
The National Autistic Society Scotland
Central Chambers, 1st Floor
109 Hope Street
Glasgow
G2 6LL
Phone: +44 (0)141 221 8090
Email: scotland@nas.org.uk
Website: www.autism.org.uk/scotland

Scottish Autism
Hilton House
Alloa Business Park
Whins Road

Alloa
FK10 3SA
Phone: +44 (0)1259 720 044
Email: autism@scottishautism.org.uk
Website: www.scottishautism.org.uk

Wales
Autism Cymru
c/o Thomas Simon Solicitors
62 Newport Road
Cardiff
CF24 0DF
Phone: +44 (0)2920 463 263
Email: Maggie@autismcymru.org
Website: www.autism-cymru.org

National Autistic Society Cymru
6–7 Village Way
Greenmeadow
Springs Business Park
Tongwynlais
Cardiff
CF15 7NE
Phone: +44 (0)2920 629 312
Email: cymru@nas.org.uk
Website: www.autism.org.uk/cymru

REPUBLIC OF IRELAND
Irish Autism Action
41 Newlands
Mullingar
Co. Westmeath
Phone: +353 (0) 44 9331609
Email: kevin1aa@ircom.net
Website: www.autismireland.ie

Irish Progressive Association for Autism
The Shine Centre
Weston View
Ballinrea Road
Carrigaline
Co. Cork
Phone: +353 (0)21 437 7052
Email: contact@shineireland.com
Website: www.shineireland.com

Irish Society for Autism
Unity Building
16/17 Lower O'Connell St
Dublin 1
Phone: +353 (01) 874 4684
Email: autism@isa.iol.ie
Website: www.autism.ie

EUROPE
Autism Europe
Rue Montoyer 39 bte 11
1000 Brussels
Belgium
Phone: +32 (0) 2 675 7505
Email: secretariat@autismeurope.org
Website: www.autismeurope.org

USA
Autism Society
4340 East-West Hwy, Suite 350
Bethesda
Maryland 20814
Phone: 301 657 0881 *or* 1 800 3AUTISM (1 800 328 8476)
Email: see form on website
Website: www.autism-society.org

CANADA
Autism Society Canada
Box 22017
1670 Heron Road
Ottawa
Ontario
K1V 0W2
Phone: (613) 789 8943
Toll-free: 1 866 476 8440
Email: info@autismsocietycanada.ca
Website: www.autismsocietycanada.ca

AUSTRALIA

Australian Advisory Board on Autism Spectrum Disorders

Street: Building 1, Level 2
14 Aquatic Drive
Frenchs Forest
NSW 2086
Postal address: PO Box 361
Forestville NSW 2087
Phone: +61 (0)2 8977 8300
Website: www.autismaus.com.au

Member organisations of Australian Advisory Board on Autism Spectrum Disorders are:

Autism Queensland Inc.
Website: www.autismqld.com.au

Autism SA
Website: www.autismsa.org.au

Autism Spectrum Australia (Aspect)
www.autismspectrum.org.au

Autism Tasmania
Website: www.autismtas.org.au

Autism Victoria trading as Amaze
Website: www.autismvictoria.org.au

Autism Association of WA
Website: www.autism.org.au

NEW ZEALAND

Autism New Zealand Inc. National Office
Level 1, Master Builders Building
271–277 Willis Street
Wellington 6011
Postal address: PO Box 6455
Marion Square
Wellington 6141
Phone: 0800 AUTISM (288 476) + 64 4 803 3501
Email: info@autismnz.org.nz
Website: www.autismnz.org.nz

Please feel free to use this page to create a personal profile of the child you live with or work with

.....................................'s **Personal Profile**

My name is ....

I am good at ....

I enjoy...

I am interested in...

My favourite things are...

I find it hard at school when.....................................

It helps me if...

I communicate my needs by.......................................

I find other children difficult to be with when............

My favourite foods are..

I cannot/do not eat ....

Things that upset me are...

If I am upset, I might..

It calms me down if...

I can help myself by..

Other people can help me by......................................